I'M ASKING THAT GOD WILL GIVE YOU CONFIDENCE TODAY. HE LOVES YOU, AND HE'S IN CHARGE!

*Why are you cast
down, O my soul,
and why are you in
turmoil within n
Hope in God; for I
again praise hi
my salvation and m*

PSALM 42:11 E

CALM IN YOUR SOUL L
CONFIDENCE IN YOUR F
TRUST GOD'S LEAD

TONY EVANS

I just want you to know that **you are seen** and cared about today. I'm praying you feel God's closeness where you need it most.

I will ask the Father, and He will give you another Helper, that He may be with you forever.

JOHN 14:16

IF WHAT YOU SEE IS ALL THAT YOU SEE, YOU DO NOT SEE ALL THERE IS TO BE SEEN BECAUSE GOD CAN MOVE ABOVE AND BEYOND THE NATURAL WORLD AND DEMONSTRATE THAT THE WORLD UP THERE CAN OVERRIDE THE LIMITATIONS DOWN HERE.

TONY EVANS

I'M PRAYING FOR GOD TO RESTORE YOUR HEART.

The Lord is near to the brokenhearted and saves the crushed in spirit.

PSALM 34:18 ESV

THE GOD WHO ALLOWS SORROWS IS ALSO THE GOD OF NEW SEASONS.

TONY EVANS

It's so natural to focus only on what we can see. But today, I'm asking God to help you to fix your eyes on Him in faith, no matter what.

The things which are seen are temporal, but the things which are not seen are eternal.

II CORINTHIANS 4:18

WHEN YOU ARE SUFFERING, LOOK FOR COMFORT FROM THAT WHICH YOU CANNOT SEE. GOD IS THE GOD OF ALL COMFORT.

TONY EVANS

I'M ASKING GOD TO REMIND YOU OF HOW MUCH HE LOVES YOU TODAY.

So we have come to know and to believe the love that God has for us. God is love, and whoever abides in love abides in God, and God abides in him.

I JOHN 4:16 ESV

YOU CAN ALWAYS TRUST GOD'S HEART EVEN WHEN YOU CAN'T UNDERSTAND HIS HAND.

TONY EVANS

I'm praying for you, asking God to draw near to you today.

Therefore let us draw near with confidence to the throne of grace, so that we may receive mercy and find grace to help in time of need.

HEBREWS 4:16

WITH JESUS, YOU HAVE BOLD ACCESS TO THE VERY PRESENCE OF GOD! IT IS YOUR GOD-GIVEN RIGHT TO DRAW NEAR TO HIM.

TONY EVANS

I'M PRAYING GOD WILL FILL YOU WITH HIS PEACE TODAY.

And the peace of God, which
surpasses all understanding,
will guard your hearts and
your minds in Christ Jesus.

PHILIPPIANS 4:7 ESV

PEACE DOESN'T MEAN THAT YOU WILL
NOT HAVE PROBLEMS. PEACE MEANS THAT
YOUR PROBLEMS WILL NOT HAVE YOU.

TONY EVANS

I'm asking God to give you the **eyes to see** yourself the way He does—in love, with joy, and recognizing the beauty of how unique you are.

For we are His workmanship, created in Christ Jesus for good works, which God prepared beforehand so that we would walk in them.

EPHESIANS 2:10

GOD CAN TAKE THE GOOD, BAD, AND THE BITTER AND CREATE A MASTERPIECE CALLED YOUR DESTINY.

TONY EVANS

I'M PRAYING THAT YOU FEEL THE INCREDIBLE GIFT OF GOD'S KINDNESS TOWARD YOU TODAY.

For His lovingkindness is great toward us,
and the truth of the Lord is everlasting.
Praise the Lord!

PSALM 117:2

YOU MAY RUN OUT OF A LOT OF THINGS IN LIFE,
BUT YOU WILL NEVER RUN OUT OF GOD'S LOVE.

TONY EVANS

I'm praying that you feel the relief of a burden lifted today.

*Cast your burden upon the Lord
and He will sustain you;
He will never allow the
righteous to be shaken.*

PSALM 55:22

MERCY RELIEVES ANOTHER PERSON'S PROBLEM.
IT LIFTS THE BURDEN. MERCY PAYS THE PRICE.

TONY EVANS

I'M PRAYING THAT YOU EXPERIENCE REAL REST TODAY, THE KIND THAT ONLY GOD CAN PROVIDE.

Take My yoke upon you and learn from Me, for I am gentle and humble in heart, and you will find rest for your souls.

MATTHEW 11:29

SOMETIMES GOD LETS YOU BE IN A SITUATION THAT ONLY HE CAN FIX SO THAT YOU CAN SEE THAT HE IS THE ONE WHO FIXES IT. REST. HE'S GOT IT.

TONY EVANS

Today I'm praying that God reminds you that He will always be with you, provide for you, and love you.

The thief comes only to steal and kill and destroy; I came that they may have life, and have it abundantly.

JOHN 10:10

GOD CAME TO GIVE YOU ABUNDANT LIFE. AND WHEN THAT RUNS OUT, HE GIVES YOU MORE AND MORE. IT NEVER ENDS, AND YOU WILL ALWAYS HAVE ENOUGH TO SHARE.

TONY EVANS

I'M PRAYING THAT YOU FEEL UPLIFTED TODAY, KNOWING THAT GOD WILL GIVE YOU WHAT YOU NEED.

Look at the birds of the air: they neither sow nor reap nor gather into barns, and yet your heavenly Father feeds them. Are you not of more value than they?

MATTHEW 6:26 ESV

GOD IS YOUR SOURCE. EVERYTHING ELSE IS JUST A RESOURCE.

TONY EVANS

I'm asking God to show you just the **right path** to take as you make this decision.

The Lord will continually guide you.

ISAIAH 58:11

GOD WILL MEET YOU WHERE YOU ARE IN ORDER TO TAKE YOU WHERE HE WANTS YOU TO GO.

TONY EVANS

I'M PRAYING THAT YOU SENSE GOD'S ACCEPTANCE OF YOU, EXACTLY AS YOU ARE.

Everyone who calls on the name of the Lord will be saved.

ROMANS 10:13 NIV

IN JESUS, YOUR DAYS AHEAD ARE GREATER THAN YOUR DAYS GONE BY.

TONY EVANS

I'm praying that you sense God's **loving care** today.

Oh give thanks to the Lord, for he is good; for his steadfast love endures forever!

I CHRONICLES 16:34 ESV

GOD HAS A GREATER PLAN
FOR THE PAIN IN YOUR LIFE.

TONY EVANS

I'M PRAYING THAT YOU'LL FEEL GOD'S COMPASSION FOR YOU TODAY.

The Lord is good to all,
And His mercies are over all His works.

PSALM 145:9

GOD ALLOWS US TO HIT ROCK
BOTTOM SO WE'LL DISCOVER THAT
HE IS THE ROCK AT THE BOTTOM.

TONY EVANS

I'm asking God to remind you that you can **trust Him fully** and wholly. Let Him take this.

The Lord will fight for you, and you have only to be silent.

EXODUS 14:14 ESV

GOD'S TIMING IS ALWAYS PERFECT. TRUST HIS DELAYS. HE'S GOT YOU.

TONY EVANS

TODAY I'M PRAYING THAT YOU WILL EXPERIENCE THE BLESSING OF GOD IN A BRAND-NEW WAY.

*The blessing of the
Lord be upon you.*

PSALM 129:8

THE GOD WHO HELPED YOU
YESTERDAY IS THE SAME GOD WHO
WILL HELP YOU TOMORROW.

TONY EVANS

I'm asking God to show you, clearly and exactly, the purpose He has called you to and the way He has designed you to truly shine.

Now there are varieties of gifts, but the same Spirit; and there are varieties of service, but the same Lord; and there are varieties of activities, but it is the same God who empowers them all in everyone.

I CORINTHIANS 12:4–6 ESV

GOD PUTS DREAMS IN YOUR HEART THAT ARE BIGGER THAN YOU SO THAT YOU WILL RELY ON HIM AND HIS POWER.

TONY EVANS

I'M PRAYING THAT YOU EXPERIENCE GOD'S GENEROSITY TODAY!

The Lord will open for you His good storehouse, the heavens, to give rain to your land in its season and to bless all the work of your hand.

DEUTERONOMY 28:12

IF GOD IS POWERFUL ENOUGH TO TAKE YOU TO HEAVEN, HE'S POWERFUL ENOUGH TO HAVE YOUR BACK ON EARTH. TRUST HIM.

TONY EVANS

God is always working. I'm praying that He will reveal His amazing ways to you today.

All things are possible with God.

MARK 10:27

GOD DOESN'T NEED A LOT TO DO A LOT.
ALL DAVID HAD WAS FIVE STONES,
AND ALL DAVID USED WAS ONE.

TONY EVANS

I ASKED GOD TO PUT YOU IN MY PATH TODAY. MY PRAYER IS THAT YOU WILL FEEL HIS LOVE AND CARE FOR YOU LIKE NEVER BEFORE.

I came that they may have life,
and have it abundantly.

JOHN 10:10

GOD KNOWS. GOD SEES.
GOD CARES. HE'S THERE.

TONY EVANS

I'm praying you'll experience God's **overflowing grace** today—so much so that you are completely overwhelmed by His love and joy.

Blessed be the God and Father of our Lord Jesus Christ, who has blessed us with every spiritual blessing in the heavenly places in Christ.

EPHESIANS 1:3

GRACE IS ALL THAT GOD IS FREE TO DO FOR YOU BECAUSE OF WHAT CHRIST HAS DONE.

TONY EVANS

I LIFTED YOU UP IN PRAYER TO THE CREATOR OF THE UNIVERSE TODAY, ASKING THAT HE WOULD POUR OUT HIS SPIRIT OF GRACE AND POWER UPON YOU.

Now to Him who is able to do far more abundantly beyond all that we ask or think, according to the power that works within us, to Him be the glory in the church and in Christ Jesus to all generations forever and ever.

EPHESIANS 3:20–21

FAITH DOESN'T MAKE SENSE.
IT MAKES MIRACLES.

TONY EVANS

You are made by God with love. He says you are **His masterpiece.** I asked Him to remind you of this fact today.

God created man in His own image, in the image of God He created him; male and female He created them.

GENESIS 1:27

YOU WERE MADE ON PURPOSE FOR A PURPOSE.

TONY EVANS

I PRAYED GOD WOULD GIVE YOU HIS STRENGTH TODAY.

He gives strength to the weary,
and to him who lacks might
He increases power.

ISAIAH 40:29

WHEN WE APPLY HEAVEN'S PERSPECTIVE
TO EARTH'S REALITIES, WE ARE ABLE
TO SOLVE EARTH'S REALITIES IN THE
WAY THEY OUGHT TO BE SOLVED.

TONY EVANS

For more kindness
resources, visit:

Today, I'm asking God to give you the peace that comes with ==trusting His plans== for you.

You will keep in perfect peace
those whose minds are steadfast,
because they trust in you.
Trust in the Lord forever,
for the Lord the Lord Himself,
is the Rock eternal.

ISAIAH 26:3–4 NIV

DO WHAT GOD HAS ALREADY SAID TO DO.
THEN WATCH HIM USHER YOU STRAIGHT OUT OF
YOUR DETOUR AND INTO YOUR DESTINY.

TONY EVANS

I PRAYED FOR GOD TO WRAP YOU IN HIS COMFORTING ARMS TODAY.

Praise be to the God and Father of our Lord Jesus Christ, the Father of compassion and the God of all comfort, who comforts us in all our troubles, so that we can comfort those in any trouble with the comfort we ourselves receive from God.

II CORINTHIANS 1:3–4 NIV

TRUST THE TRUTH YOU KNOW—THE TRUTH THAT GOD CARES ENOUGH ABOUT YOU TO CARE FOR YOU IN ANY AND EVERY WAY YOU NEED HIM TO.

TONY EVANS

For more kindness
resources, visit:

I prayed for you to have a great day!

Rejoice in the Lord always; again I will say, rejoice! Let your gentle spirit be known to all men. The Lord is near.

PHILIPPIANS 4:4–5

WE ARE PUT ON EARTH TO LIVE LIFE TO THE FULL, BECAUSE THIS IS THE ONLY CHANCE WE GET TO DO IT.

TONY EVANS

TODAY I'M THANKING GOD FOR YOU—THE WAY HE DESIGNED YOU, AND THE WAY HE PLACED YOU IN MY LIFE.

As each one has received a special gift, employ it in serving one another as good stewards of the manifold grace of God.

I PETER 4:10

THE DEGREE TO WHICH YOU CONNECT EVERYTHING IN YOUR LIFE TO CHRIST IS THE DEGREE TO WHICH YOU WILL EXPERIENCE EVERYTHING GOD WANTS YOU TO HAVE FROM CHRIST.

TONY EVANS

I prayed that you would find comfort knowing that you have a perfect place in God's perfect design.

So then you are no longer strangers and aliens, but you are fellow citizens with the saints, and are of God's household.

EPHESIANS 2:19

GOD DOESN'T WANT YOU TO MERELY BE A RESERVOIR TO RECEIVE HIS BLESSING, BUT ALSO AN AQUEDUCT TO CONVEY IT.

TONY EVANS

I PRAYED THAT TODAY YOU WOULD ENJOY ALL THAT GOD HAS PROVIDED FOR YOU IN YOUR LIFE.

As for every person to whom God has given riches and wealth, He has also given him the opportunity to enjoy them and to receive his reward and rejoice in his labor; this is the gift of God.

ECCLESIASTES 5:19 NASB

YOU DON'T HAVE TO FEEL GUILTY ABOUT THE GOD-GIVEN THINGS YOU HAVE. GOD EXPECTS YOU TO ENJOY THE GOOD THINGS IN LIFE, THANKING HIM FOR HIS PROVISION.

TONY EVANS

For more kindness
resources, visit:

I'm praying that you experience God's goodness **in abundance** today.

The Lord is good to all, and his mercy is over all that he has made.

PSALM 145:9 ESV

THE HOLY SPIRIT KNOWS WHAT YOU NEED AND WHEN YOU NEED IT.

TONY EVANS

I'M PRAYING THAT GOD'S LOVE WOULD OVERFLOW IN YOUR LIFE TODAY!

Be devoted to one another in brotherly love; give preference to one another in honor.

ROMANS 12:10

LOVE IS A BADGE WE CHOOSE TO WEAR EVERY DAY.

TONY EVANS

I'm asking God to make His comfort very clear to you today. May you feel His embrace and love.

For just as the sufferings of Christ are ours in abundance, so also our comfort is abundant through Christ.

II CORINTHIANS 1:5

NO MATTER WHAT, KEEP LIVING BECAUSE GOD PROMISES COMFORT IN ANY SITUATION, AND HE WILL COME ALONGSIDE YOU TO HELP.

TONY EVANS

I'M PRAYING THAT WORDS OF ENCOURAGEMENT WOULD REACH YOU TODAY AND THAT GOD WOULD STRENGTHEN YOUR HEART.

May grace and peace be multiplied to you in the knowledge of God and of Jesus our Lord.

II PETER 1:2 ESV

JESUS IS NEVER MORE REAL TO YOU THAN IN THOSE TIMES WHEN LIFE DOES NOT SEEM TO BE WORKING OUT.

TONY EVANS

I'm praying today that you will be content, embracing all that God has given you— and joyfully anticipating His future grace.

I have learned in whatever situation I am to be content... I have learned the secret of facing plenty and hunger, abundance and need. I can do all things through him who strengthens me.

PHILIPPIANS 4:11–13 ESV

CONTENTMENT IS A DISCOVERY. IT'S A PROCESS OF LEARNING TO BE AT EASE WITH WHERE YOU ARE AND WITH WHAT THE LORD HAS PROVIDED TO YOU.

TONY EVANS

I PRAYED THAT YOU WOULD EXPERIENCE GOD'S PEACE TODAY— AND BE INSPIRED TO PASS IT ON.

Blessed are the peacemakers,
for they shall be called sons of God.

MATTHEW 5:9

SOMEONE WHO IS WILLING TO BE
A PEACEMAKER IS SOMEONE WHO
CARRIES THE KINGDOM OF GOD.

TONY EVANS

I'm praying that God's care for you would be unmistakable today.

> Say to those who have
> an anxious heart,
> "Be strong; fear not!
> Behold, your God
> will come with vengeance,
> with the recompense of God.
> He will come and save you."

ISAIAH 35:4 ESV

ALLOW YOUR PAIN TO BRING YOU TO A PLACE
WHERE YOU RECEIVE AND LIVE OUT YOUR
PURPOSE. LEARN FROM IT. GROW.

TONY EVANS

I'M PRAYING THAT YOU WILL FEEL GOD'S PRESENCE AS YOU FACE TODAY'S CHALLENGES.

Consider it all joy, my brethren, when you encounter various trials, knowing that the testing of your faith produces endurance.

JAMES 1:2–3

PEOPLE WOULD RATHER GO STRAIGHT FROM DELIVERANCE INTO DESTINY. BUT THE IN-BETWEEN TIME IS ACTUALLY DESIGNED TO DEVELOP YOU IN PREPARATION FOR THAT DESTINY.

TONY EVANS

I'm praying that you feel the **love and care** of those around you. God values you so deeply!

God decided in advance to adopt us into his own family by bringing us to himself through Jesus Christ.

EPHESIANS 1:5 NLT

GOD HASN'T EQUIPPED YOU TO FULFILL SOMEONE ELSE'S DESTINY. HE HAS A DESTINY JUST FOR YOU.

TONY EVANS

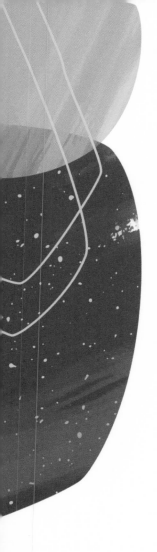

I'M PRAYING TODAY THAT YOU WILL CONNECT WITH GOD AND KNOW THAT HE HEARS YOU.

But truly God has listened;
he has attended to the
voice of my prayer.

PSALM 66:19 ESV

PRAYER IS ONE OF YOUR
GREATEST TOOLS IN THE BATTLE
AGAINST THE EVIL ONE.

TONY EVANS

I'm praying that you will see that nothing in your life is by accident; **God is leading you** through it all.

The lot is cast into the lap,
but its every decision is from the Lord.

PROVERBS 16:33 ESV

GOD WANTS YOU TO SEE HIM IN THE SILENCE.

TONY EVANS

I'M PRAYING YOU SENSE GOD'S CLOSENESS TODAY. HE IS NEVER TOO FAR FROM YOU.

The steadfast of mind You will keep in perfect peace, Because he trusts in You.

ISAIAH 26:3

FOCUSING ON GOD TAKES YOU OUT OF FOCUSING ON WHERE YOU ARE, TO WHO HE IS.

TONY EVANS

For more kindness
resources, visit:

I'm praying that **God will give you wisdom** for whatever decisions you need to make today.

If any of you lacks wisdom, let him ask God, who gives generously to all without reproach, and it will be given him.

JAMES 1:5 ESV

WISDOM IS THE WAY TO EXPERIENCE GOD'S WILL AND HIS FAVOR BECAUSE WISDOM IS THE APPLICATION OF GOD'S WILL TO THE PRACTICAL AREAS OF LIFE.

TONY EVANS

I'M ASKING GOD TO LEAD YOU IN YOUR PARTICULAR ROLE SO THAT YOU THRIVE IN IT!

He has told you, O man, what is good;
and what does the Lord require of you
but to do justice, and to love kindness,
and to walk humbly with your God?

MICAH 6:8 ESV

NOT EVERYONE HAS THE SAME JOB OR
THE SAME NOTORIETY, BUT EVERYBODY
IS CRITICAL AND VALUABLE.

TONY EVANS

I'm praying for you today. May God's peace —the kind that goes beyond anything that makes sense—settle your heart today.

Peace I leave with you; My peace I give to you; not as the world gives do I give to you. Do not let your heart be troubled, nor let it be fearful.

JOHN 14:27

DON'T START WITH GOD THEN END WITH YOUR MOUNTAIN. START WITH YOUR MOUNTAIN THEN END WITH GOD SO HE WILL HAVE THE FINAL WORD OVER YOUR SITUATION.

TONY EVANS

I PRAYED TODAY THAT YOU WOULD CAST YOUR CARES UPON JESUS BECAUSE HE CARES FOR YOU.

Humble yourselves, therefore, under the mighty hand of God so that at the proper time he may exalt you, casting all your anxieties on him, because he cares for you.

I PETER 5:6–7 ESV

ASK GOD FOR THE GRACE YOU NEED TO FACE THE CHALLENGES UP AHEAD. THEN LOOK TO HIM AND HIS HAND TO GUIDE YOU.

TONY EVANS

I'm asking God to give you **patience** and **understanding** today. He is holding on to you.

He who dwells in the shelter
of the Most High
will abide in the shadow
of the Almighty.

PSALM 91:1 ESV

TESTING TIMES ARE NEVER WHAT WE
CHOOSE, BUT THEY LEAD TO THE ABUNDANCE
THAT ALLOWS US TO WORSHIP HIM MORE
PURELY AND LOVE OTHERS MORE FULLY.

TONY EVANS

I'M ASKING GOD TO REMIND YOU, IN SPECIAL AND OBVIOUS WAYS, JUST HOW MUCH HE LOVES YOU.

For I am sure that neither death nor life, nor angels nor rulers, nor things present nor things to come, nor powers, nor height nor depth, nor anything else in all creation, will be able to separate us from the love of God in Christ Jesus our Lord.

ROMANS 8:38–39 ESV

LOVE IS THE KEY TO GOD'S HOUSE, WHERE YOU CAN GO ANYTIME YOU WANT AS ONE OF HIS CHILDREN. LOVE UNITES US, DISTINGUISHES US, AND LIGHTS THE WAY TO OUR DESTINY WITH HIM.

TONY EVANS

I'm praying that you will release all your troubles to God today. He can handle them!

> *Ah, Lord God! It is you who have made the heavens and the earth by your great power and by your outstretched arm! Nothing is too hard for you.*
>
> **JEREMIAH 32:17 ESV**

A BIG PROBLEM JUST MEANS THAT GOD CAN OFFER A BIGGER SOLUTION.

TONY EVANS

I'M PRAYING THAT YOU'LL GO TO GOD WITH EVERYTHING ON YOUR MIND TODAY. HE IS LISTENING!

But when you pray, go into your room and shut the door and pray to your Father who is in secret. And your Father who sees in secret will reward you.

MATTHEW 6:6 ESV

DON'T WORRY THAT YOU MAY PRAY POORLY. WORRY IF YOU DON'T PRAY AT ALL. JUST PRAY. IT DOESN'T HAVE TO BE PERFECT.

TONY EVANS

I'm praying today that you would rest in the fact that **God has designed you** for His purpose.

But to each one is given the manifestation of the Spirit for the common good.

I CORINTHIANS 12:7

GOD MOVES THROUGH CONNECTION, BOTH VERTICAL AND HORIZONTAL. DRAWING NEAR TO HIM IS ESSENTIAL. BUT SO IS REACHING OUT TO OTHERS.

TONY EVANS

I'M PRAYING TODAY THAT YOU WOULD EXPERIENCE THE DEPTH OF GOD'S COMPASSION FOR YOU.

In everything, therefore, treat people the same way you want them to treat you.

MATTHEW 7:12

GOD LETS YOU GO THROUGH SOME THINGS SO THAT YOU WILL UNDERSTAND WHAT OTHERS ARE GOING THROUGH.

TONY EVANS

I'm praying the Lord would overwhelm you with His love today.

We love, because He first loved us.

I JOHN 4:19

WHEN WE LOVE, GOD'S LOVE BURSTS OUT ON US.

TONY EVANS

I'M ASKING GOD TO BLESS YOU TODAY—AND THAT YOU WOULD BE INSPIRED TO PASS ON THE BLESSING!

All the believers were one in heart and mind. No one claimed that any of their possessions was their own, but they shared everything they had.

ACTS 4:32 NIV

SHARING IS NO SMALL THING BECAUSE IT IS ROOTED IN THE THEOLOGY OF THE FAITH: "FOR GOD SO LOVED THE WORLD THAT HE GAVE."

TONY EVANS

I'm praying that the God of peace will give you great hope today.

In the world you have tribulation, but take courage; I have overcome the world.

JOHN 16:33

THE TEMPTATION IN YOUR TEARS IS TO GIVE UP ON GOD. BUT TRUST HIM, EVEN IN THE DARK. HE IS UP TO SOMETHING GOOD.

TONY EVANS

I'M PRAYING THAT YOU WILL EXPERIENCE THE POWER OF GOD'S HELP TODAY.

God is our refuge and strength,
A very present help in trouble.

PSALM 46:1

When God puts you in a situation you cannot fix no matter how much money you have or intelligence you have or power you possess, He is doing you a favor. He is showing you your insufficiency so that you can see the kingdom of heaven at work on your behalf.

TONY EVANS

One step at a time, friend. I'm praying for you.

Your word is a lamp to my feet And a light to my path.

PSALM 119:105

WHEN CIRCUMSTANCES ARE PILING ON TOP OF YOU, SHAKE THEM OFF AND TAKE A STEP. ONE STEP AT A TIME. AND NEXT THING YOU KNOW, YOU'LL BE STEPPING INTO YOUR PROMISED LAND.

TONY EVANS

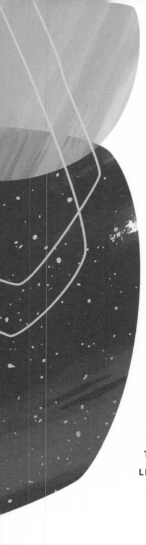

I'M ASKING GOD TO REMIND YOU THAT HE IS THE ARCHITECT OF YOUR FUTURE.

For I know the plans I have for you, declares the Lord, plans for welfare and not for evil, to give you a future and a hope. Then you will call upon me and come and pray to me, and I will hear you. You will seek me and find me, when you seek me with all your heart.

JEREMIAH 29:11–13 ESV

THE WAY YOU GET TO SEE THE PLAN FOR YOUR LIFE IS IN YOUR RELATIONSHIP TO THE PLANNER. PURSUE GOD. HE WILL SHOW YOU THE PLAN.

TONY EVANS

For more kindness
resources, visit:

I'm praying that you will trust in God—and that He will reveal His heart to you.

Trust in the Lord with all your heart
And do not lean on your
own understanding.
In all your ways acknowledge Him,
And He will make straight your paths.

PROVERBS 3:5–6

LOOK FOR GOD'S PRESENCE IN SPITE OF
THE PROBLEM YOU FACE, AND YOU WILL
DISCOVER HE IS WITH YOU EVEN WHEN
THINGS DON'T ALWAYS MAKE SENSE.

TONY EVANS

I'M PRAYING TODAY
THAT YOU WILL EXPERIENCE
GOD'S GENEROSITY —AND
BE INSPIRED TO PASS IT ON!

The generous man will be prosperous,
And he who waters will himself be watered.

PROVERBS 11:25

WHEN YOUR RESOURCES BEGIN TO RUN
DRY, TURN TO THE ULTIMATE SOURCE,
AND RELY ON HIM TO PROVIDE.

TONY EVANS

DaySpring

I prayed for you today. I want you to know that **God is with you** and will never leave you.

And behold, I am with you always, to the end of the age.

MATTHEW 28:20 ESV

WHEN YOU ARE IN GOD'S WILL, NO ONE CAN HAVE WHAT BELONGS TO YOU.

TONY EVANS

I'M PRAYING YOU WOULD EXPERIENCE THE TRUE JOY AND RELEASE OF FORGIVENESS HOWEVER YOU NEED IT.

Judge not, and you will not be judged; condemn not, and you will not be condemned; forgive, and you will be forgiven; give, and it will be given to you.

LUKE 6:37–38 ESV

FORGIVENESS UNCOLLARS YOU FROM BITTERNESS, ANGER, RESENTMENT, WRATH, REVENGE, AND ALL OF THE LINKS IN A CHAIN CALLED UNFORGIVENESS.

TONY EVANS

I'm asking God to make sure you know how very appreciated you are!

Share with the Lord's people who are in need. Practice hospitality.

ROMANS 12:13 NIV

HOSPITALITY IS ABOUT THE MEETING OF NEEDS AND THE SHOWING OF LOVE IN GOD'S WAY.

TONY EVANS

I'M PRAYING THAT YOUR HEART WOULD BE FILLED WITH GRATITUDE AND A RENEWED SENSE OF PURPOSE TODAY.

Give thanks in all circumstances;
for this is the will of God in
Christ Jesus for you.

I THESSALONIANS 5:18 ESV

YOU RARELY SEE PEOPLE
WHO KNOW THEIR PURPOSE
LIVING A MISERABLE LIFE.

TONY EVANS

For more kindness
resources, visit:

Today I'm asking God to give you boldness and a refreshed spirit.

Have I not commanded you? Be strong and courageous. Do not be frightened, and do not be dismayed, for the Lord your God is with you wherever you go.

JOSHUA 1:9 ESV

IT TAKES COURAGE TO STAND OUT FOR PEACE.

TONY EVANS

For more kindness
resources, visit:

TODAY I'M ASKING GOD TO ENCOURAGE YOUR HEART AND WARM YOUR SPIRIT WITH EVERY BLESSING IN HIM.

Blessed are the poor in spirit, for theirs is the kingdom of heaven.

MATTHEW 5:3

WHEN YOU PROTECT YOUR HEART AND KEEP IT UNDIVIDED, THEN YOU WILL SEE GOD INTERVENE IN YOUR CIRCUMSTANCES. YOU WILL SEE GOD FOR YOURSELF.

TONY EVANS

I'm praying that your heart and God's will connect in a special way today.

Let your roots grow down into him, and let your lives be built on Him. Then your faith will grow strong in the truth you were taught, and you will overflow with thankfulness.

COLOSSIANS 2:7 NLT

GOD DOESN'T WANT YOU TO BE A SHIP, BOUNCED AND TOSSED BY THE WAVES. HE WANTS YOU TO BE A SUBMARINE, WITH SOMETHING DEEP INSIDE THAT DOESN'T DEPEND ON WHAT'S HAPPENING ON THE OUTSIDE.

TONY EVANS

I'M PRAYING THAT YOU EXPERIENCE GOD'S REAL LOVE FOR YOU SO THAT IT FILLS YOU UP WITH JOY.

There is no fear in love; but perfect love casts out fear, because fear involves punishment, and the one who fears is not perfected in love.

I JOHN 4:18

GOD IS ON YOUR SIDE.

TONY EVANS

I'm asking God to give you a glimpse of what He is up to so that you will be encouraged.

Surely there is a future,
and your hope will not be cut off.

PROVERBS 23:18 ESV

REGARDLESS OF WHAT HAPPENED YESTERDAY, IF YOU STICK WITH THE LORD TODAY, YOUR YESTERDAY DOESN'T HAVE TO CONTROL YOUR TOMORROW.

TONY EVANS

I'M PRAYING YOU FIND COMFORT TODAY WHERE YOU NEED IT AND HOPE FOR A NEW TOMORROW.

*Come to Me, all who are
weary and heavy-laden,
and I will give you rest.*

MATTHEW 11:28

MORE THAN YOUR TIME OR TALENT,
JESUS WANTS YOUR HEART.

TONY EVANS

For more kindness
resources, visit:

I know you've got a lot going on, and I want you to know that you are being prayed for through it all. **May God's peace be with you!**

For the kingdom of God is not eating and drinking, but righteousness and peace and joy in the Holy Spirit.

ROMANS 14:17

GOD BLESSES US WITH AN INNER PEACE AND JOY—AN OVERALL INNER WELL-BEING THAT GIVES US THE SUSTENANCE WE NEED.

TONY EVANS

I'M ASKING GOD TO GIVE YOU A RENEWED SENSE OF PURPOSE IN YOUR WORK TODAY.

Whatever you do, work heartily, as for the Lord and not for men, knowing that from the Lord you will receive the inheritance as your reward. You are serving the Lord Christ.

COLOSSIANS 3:23–24 ESV

EVERY JOB MATTERS. THERE ARE NO BIG "I'S" AND LITTLE "YOU'S" IN THE FAMILY OF GOD.

TONY EVANS

My prayer for you today is that you will feel the presence of God with you during every challenge you face.

Even though I walk through the valley of the shadow of death, I will fear no evil, for you are with me; your rod and your staff, they comfort me.

PSALM 23:4 ESV

YOUR GREATEST LESSONS IN FAITH ARE OFTEN LEARNED IN THE DARK.

TONY EVANS

I'M PRAYING THAT YOU FEEL FULFILLMENT AND PEACE NO MATTER WHAT THE DAY BRINGS.

Now may the Lord of peace himself give you peace at all times in every way. The Lord be with you all.

II THESSALONIANS 3:16 ESV

PAIN IS ALWAYS AN INVITATION TO PRAY.

TONY EVANS

I'm asking God to **fill you up today** and bless you in a big way.

God is able to make all grace abound to you, so that always having all sufficiency in everything, you may have an abundance for every good deed.

II CORINTHIANS 9:8

GOD WANTS YOU TO TRUST HIS TIMING. HE'S GOT IT ALL COMING TOGETHER. WALK BY FAITH.

TONY EVANS

I'M ASKING GOD TO COMFORT YOU TODAY WITH THE KNOWLEDGE THAT HE SEES, HE KNOWS, AND HE CARES.

The God of peace will soon crush Satan under your feet. The grace of our Lord Jesus Christ be with you.

ROMANS 16:20

STANDING FIRM IN THE ARMOR OF GOD DOESN'T STOP THE SPIRITUAL WARFARE FROM RAGING. IT STOPS IT FROM DEFEATING YOU.

TONY EVANS

I'm thanking God for you today and asking Him to refresh your spirit.

Let us hold fast the confession of our hope without wavering, for he who promised is faithful.

HEBREWS 10:23 ESV

GOD MAY NOT GET YOU OUT OF A DETOUR WHEN YOU WANT HIM TO, BUT HE WILL JUMP IN THE CAR AND JOIN YOU. YOU ARE NEVER ALONE.

TONY EVANS

I'M ASKING THAT GOD WILL GIVE YOU THE ENDURANCE TO WAIT AS HIS PERFECT PLAN FOR YOU IS FULFILLED.

And after you have suffered a little while, the God of all grace, who has called you to his eternal glory in Christ, will himself restore, confirm, strengthen, and establish you.

I PETER 5:10 ESV

WHEN GOD IS READY TO MOVE,
IT WON'T TAKE LONG.

TONY EVANS

Do you know how deeply loved you are? I'm asking God to make it very clear to you today.

For God so loved the world, that He gave His only begotten Son, that whoever believes in Him shall not perish, but have eternal life.

JOHN 3:16

AT THE CROSS, SATAN DIDN'T LOSE HIS POWER. HE LOST HIS AUTHORITY. HE CAN'T RULE YOU. HE JUST WANTS YOU TO THINK HE CAN.

TONY EVANS

I'M PRAYING THAT YOUR EYES WILL BE OPENED TO THE BEAUTY THAT GOD HAS EMBEDDED IN THIS DAY.

This is the day which the Lord has made;
Let us rejoice and be glad in it.

PSALM 118:24

YOU CAN GO A LONG WAY WITH
A CHANGE IN YOUR PERSPECTIVE,
RATHER THAN BE STUCK WAITING ON
A CHANGE IN YOUR CIRCUMSTANCE.

TONY EVANS

I'm praying that you trust in the God who made you **on purpose, for a purpose.**

For it is God who is at work in you, both to will and to work for His good pleasure.

PHILIPPIANS 2:13

GOD MADE YOU UNIQUE ON PURPOSE. HE HAS A PLAN THAT ONLY YOUR PERSONALITY, BACKGROUND, TEMPERAMENT, MINDSET, AND SKILLS CAN FULFILL. BE COOL WITH YOU!

TONY EVANS

I'M ASKING GOD TO REMIND YOU THAT HE IS FOR YOU.

*Then my enemies will turn back
in the day when I call;
This I know, that God is for me.*

PSALM 56:9

YOU ARE NOT FIGHTING FOR
VICTORY IN SPIRITUAL BATTLES.
YOU ARE FIGHTING FROM VICTORY.
CHRIST HAS SECURED THE OUTCOME.
REMAIN STRONG IN FAITH.

TONY EVANS

I'm praying that you will **experience freedom** from past hang-ups and rejoice in the goodness of God today.

It was for freedom that Christ set us free.
GALATIANS 5:1

WHEN YOU REALLY RECOGNIZE GOD'S GOODNESS, YOU WANT TO SERVE HIM. SERVING GOD BECOMES A PASSION, AN OPPORTUNITY, AND A PRIVILEGE.
TONY EVANS

I'M PRAYING THAT GOD WILL GIVE YOU THE ENDURANCE AND HOPE TO KEEP MOVING FORWARD.

Let us run with endurance the race that is set before us, looking to Jesus, the founder and perfecter of our faith.

HEBREWS 12:1–2 ESV

SATAN WANTS TO KEEP YOU LOOKING BACK SO HE CAN KEEP YOU FROM MOVING FORWARD.

TONY EVANS

For more kindness
resources, visit:

I'm praying today that you feel **loved, supported,** and as **blessed** as you truly are.

You hem me in, behind and before, and lay your hand upon me.

PSALM 139:5 ESV

TAKE A MOMENT AND LET [GOD] KNOW THAT YOU RECOGNIZE HOW KIND HE HAS BEEN TO YOU.

TONY EVANS

I'M ASKING GOD TO SUSTAIN YOU TODAY AND GIVE YOU A GLIMPSE OF THE GOOD THAT IS TO COME.

Blessed be the God and Father of our Lord Jesus Christ, who has blessed us with every spiritual blessing in the heavenly places in Christ.

EPHESIANS 1:3

WALK HUMBLY WITH GOD, AND TRUST HIS PROCESS. WHEN YOU DO, HE WILL POUR OUT HIS BLESSINGS.

TONY EVANS

I'm praying that you will trust God and see His good provision for you at just the right time, in all the right ways.

Do not be afraid, little flock,
for your Father has chosen gladly
to give you the kingdom.

LUKE 12:32

WITH GOD, EVERY ALLOTTED
THING THAT GOD HAS
DECLARED FOR YOU IS IN
THE HEAVENLY REALMS, AND
IT WILL COME TO YOU.

TONY EVANS

I'M ASKING GOD TO BLESS YOU TODAY IN THE WAYS THAT YOU'LL FEEL IT MOST.

*The Lord bless you and keep you;
the Lord make his face to shine upon
you and be gracious to you;
the Lord lift up his countenance
upon you and give you peace.*

NUMBERS 6:24–26 ESV

FAITH IS CONFIDENCE
IN THE INTEGRITY OF GOD.

TONY EVANS

I'm praying that
God would meet all
your needs today
according to His divine
purpose for you.

And my God will supply every
need of yours according to his
riches in glory in Christ Jesus.
PHILIPPIANS 4:19 ESV

GOD HAS A DIVINE INTERSECTION WHERE YOUR
NEEDS AND HIS DIVINE WILL COLLIDE TOGETHER.
TONY EVANS

I'M PRAYING THAT YOU WILL FIND TOTAL PEACE IN GOD'S STRENGTH TODAY.

Submit yourselves therefore to God. Resist the devil, and he will flee from you. Draw near to God, and he will draw near to you.

JAMES 4:7–8 ESV

THE ABSENCE OF SURRENDER TO GOD BRINGS CHAOS. THE PRESENCE OF SURRENDER TO GOD BRINGS CALM.

TONY EVANS

I'm praying today that God will refresh your heart and renew your strength.

But they who wait for the Lord
shall renew their strength;
they shall mount up with
wings like eagles;
they shall run and not be weary;
they shall walk and not faint.

ISAIAH 40:31 ESV

WHATEVER MAY BE, GOD CAN TAKE YOUR
DEAD OR DYING SCENARIO AND CALL FORTH A
RESURRECTION. HE CAN TAKE WHAT LOOKS LIKE
A ROTTING SITUATION AND GIVE IT NEW LIFE.

TONY EVANS

I'M PRAYING FOR YOU TODAY, ASKING GOD TO HEAL YOUR HURTS AND HELP YOU FIND RELEASE AND RELIEF.

Be kind to one another, tender-hearted, forgiving each other, just as God in Christ also has forgiven you.

EPHESIANS 4:32

FORGIVENESS GIVES YOU THE TOOLS NEEDED TO HEAL AND MOVE ON, RELEASING THE OTHER PERSON FOR YOUR BENEFIT.

TONY EVANS

My prayer for you today is that God will give you **peace that silences your fears.**

Peace I leave with you; my peace I give to you. Not as the world gives do I give to you. Let not your hearts be troubled, neither let them be afraid.

JOHN 14:27 ESV

YOU WILL KNOW GOD HEARD YOUR PRAYER, NOT BECAUSE YOUR PROBLEM HAS BEEN SOLVED. YOU KNOW GOD HAS HEARD YOUR PRAYER BECAUSE OF THE PEACE HE GIVES YOU.

TONY EVANS

I'M PRAYING FOR GOD'S HAND OF MERCY TO RELIEVE AND COMFORT YOU IN EVERY WAY.

But God, being rich in mercy, because of the great love with which he loved us, even when we were dead in our trespasses, made us alive together with Christ—by grace you have been saved.

EPHESIANS 2:4–5 ESV

NOT EVERYTHING THAT WEIGHS YOU DOWN IS YOURS TO CARRY.

TONY EVANS

I'm asking God
that He will make you
unshakable in spirit
today.

For the righteous will never be moved;
he will be remembered forever.
He is not afraid of bad news;
his heart is firm, trusting in the Lord.

PSALM 112:6–7 ESV

PEACE IS WELL-BEING DESPITE
THE CIRCUMSTANCES.

TONY EVANS

I'M ASKING GOD
TO LEAD YOU WELL,
KEEP YOU CLOSE,
AND SHOW YOU HOW
MUCH HE CARES.

Whoever drinks of the water that I will give him shall never thirst; but the water that I will give him will become in him a well of water springing up to eternal life.

JOHN 4:14

HOPE IS ALWAYS AN OPTION.

TONY EVANS

Today I'm asking God to remind you that you are **fearfully and wonderfully made.**

I will give thanks to You, for I am fearfully and wonderfully made; Wonderful are Your works, And my soul knows it very well.

PSALM 139:14

IF YOU ARE NOT HAPPY WITH WHO YOU ARE, YOU HAVE NOT YET DISCOVERED WHO GOD CREATED YOU TO BE.

TONY EVANS